MW01277250

For The
Airline Passenger

Passenger Questions &
Pilot Answers

by
John Cronin

If you have a question about flying that is not in this booklet, send it to me and perhaps I'll answer it in a second booklet.

Please send all inquiries to:
John Cronin
PO Box 1204
Edison, NJ 08818-1204

If you want a response, please send a self-addressed stamped envelope.

Thanks to:

Sylvia Schachter
Alan Schachter
Rich Yourstone
Sherrie Yourstone

Library of Congress Catalog Number: 94-96763
ISBN 0-9648365-4-8

Greetings,

I decided to write this booklet after a passenger asked me some questions about flying. I realized then that passengers are very curious about what they see and hear around them on the plane. My answers to the questions were written to be understood by the average traveler. I left out most of the technical jargon and mathematics. I explained some topics in a most basic sense. This booklet is not meant to be instructional. It is meant to give insight to the world of air transportation.

Bear in mind that every airplane is different; every pilot has different techniques, and every airline and airport has different procedures. Just because something doesn't happen the way I explain in this booklet doesn't mean it's wrong. Always follow the instructions of the flight crew, as well as airline and airport personnel. I hope you enjoy this booklet.

John Cronin

My background:

> Captain, EMB-120 Brasilia
> Airline Transport Pilot license
> Flight Engineer-Boeing 727-200
> Certified Flight Instructor
> More than 1,000 hours of flight instruction given.
> More than five years flying at an airline.
> Air Force Reserve Captain
> BS Aviation Management/Flight Training
> Worked six months as a baggage handler.

For my parents, John and Marian.
Their support and encouragement
for my dreams knew no bounds.

CONTENTS

Air Traffic Control (ATC)

Pilots

Airports

Airplanes

49)   Why do planes get near the destination then divert to another airport? *page 59*

50)   How is my pet handled? *page 60*

DO YOU NEED A GIFT FOR A PILOT?

On the following page is a poem I wrote one night in Chicago. I put it on a plaque which makes for a unique gift. I make each one myself and it takes about a day to make eight of them. When complete, I sign the back and date it. Each plaque is numbered and has my mailing address. It is shipped US Mail and will arrive wrapped in tissue paper in a gift box. The plaque measures about 7½ X 10 inches. It has a hole drilled in the back for easy hanging. If you would like to purchase one, please send $20.00 plus $3.00 postage. Save $5.00 when you send the bar code from the back of this book (no copies please). Please allow a few weeks for delivery. If you're not satisfied, send it back and I'll refund your $20.00 (or $15.00 if you used the bar code). Thank you!!!

A DREAM TO FLY

John Cronin

It's in your blood; you don't know why
Just one goal; you've got to fly

To feel your craft; take to flight
Its' been your dream; 'most every night

Then it came; your first flight
You spread your wings; it sure felt right

Above the ground; so high and free
You could only think; it's meant to be

Ground school, flight school; summer and fall
So many lessons; to learn it all

Stalls and spins; and the lazy 8
You love to fly; but these you hate

Private, commercial; then ATP
A lot of work; you'll come to see

To build up time; you must agree
You'd fly anything; you'd fly for free

Snow streaks by; in your lights
What a show; this cold winter night

Rain at the airport; dark and cold
Breakout on top; a sight to behold

Cloud gives way; the storm is past
The air is smooth; your plane is fast

See the mountains; and oceans too
So many places; you'll pass through

Slice through clouds; on silver wings
So magnificent; to see these things

Props and jets; big and small
Coast to coast; you'll see it all

It's in your blood; you don't know why
You just can't stop; you've got to fly

1)   Why do we taxi onto the runway and then not move for
      awhile?

Sometimes the air traffic controller will issue an instruction to the
pilot to *taxi into position and hold*. This means to taxi onto the
runway and align the aircraft in the direction of departure. Then
the aircraft is to stop and hold its position. This clearance is
given when the aircraft that just landed is still on the runway. It
is also given when other airplanes are taxiing across the runway.
It's also possible that an intersecting runway is in use.
Sometimes, the controller has to provide more than usual space
between the previous departure and your aircraft. This is
especially true when the previous departure was a large aircraft
like the Boeing 747. In this case, the delay is to allow the
previous aircraft's wake turbulence to dissipate.

2)   Exactly what is a holding pattern?

Holding patterns are used when airport operations are suddenly,
and temporarily, suspended. This may occur because the
President of the United States is flying in or out of the airport.
An airport may close to allow for snow removal or there may be
an emergency situation. Holding patterns can also be used when
there are too many airplanes and the *system* gets backed up. A
pilot might *hold* to work on a mechanical problem or wait for the
weather to improve.

A holding pattern has a racetrack shape when there is no wind.
There are speed limits and pilots generally slow down enroute to
the holding location. A standard holding pattern for a jet above
14,000 feet would be conducted at less than 265 knots (305
MPH), use right turns and timing on the straight legs of 1-1/2
minutes. Most pilots will ask for legs of ten or more miles.

There may be several other aircraft in the holding pattern at the same time. They will each be at a different altitude. Pilots are given a time at which they may expect to be released. Depending on the reason for the holding, the amount of time expected to hold, and the amount of fuel on board, a pilot may elect to go immediately to an alternate airport or to hold as long as fuel allows and then proceed to an alternate.

3)   Are there speed limits?

Yes. Below 10,000 feet, the limit is 250 knots (288 MPH). In an airport traffic area, it's 200 knots (230 MPH). There are also limits for holding patterns. It depends on altitude and whether or not the airplane is a jet.

4)   What guidance does ATC provide?

The first controller of a flight is the ground controller. He is responsible for all movement on the airport, even automobiles or fire trucks that are out of the ramp area. He tells the pilot what runway to taxi to and the route to take. The next controller is the tower controller. He is responsible for flights in the airport traffic area: from the surface of the airport to 2,500 feet and out to 5 miles. This controller issues take-off and landing clearances.

After take-off, the pilot contacts departure control. The flight is now under radar guidance. The departure controller will climb the plane to an initial altitude and head it for the first navigational fix of the route. This controller knows each flight that is about to depart from several airports in the area and where they need to go. This controller will get the planes out of the area without conflict to arriving flights.

The next controller will get the flight established on the route. At this point, the flight may be 40 miles from the departure airport.

Finally, the pilot will communicate with a *center*. Twenty-one centers control all the high altitude airspace in the United States. For example, Boston Center owns the airspace from Long Island Sound to Canada, from the coast to western New York State. Boston Center, like all centers, is a large windowless building with controllers sitting at radar screens. By the way, Boston Center is located near a highway in Nashua, New Hampshire.

As the plane cruises, the pilot may talk to one or more controllers at the same center as he passes through their airspace. If he flies far enough, he will be handed off to the next center. He may talk to Boston Center, then Cleveland Center and Chicago Center until he has flown to his destination area.

Eventually, the controller will descend the airplane as it nears the destination. This may begin about 100-150 miles away. The *center* controller will hand the flight over to a local controller who will pass it to approach control.

Approach control will sequence the flights into something like a long convoy. All the planes are spaced to allow time for the previous arrival to approach, to land and taxi clear of the runway. Approach control will establish the flights on the final approach course and then hand them off to the tower controller. Again, the tower controller issues the landing and take-off clearances. After landing, the airplane will once again be guided by the ground controller until its arrival at the ramp/gate area.

5)   What do pilots carry in those square-like black cases?

They carry mostly air charts and approach plates.   Approach plates are navigational diagrams for a specific type of approach to a specific runway at a specific airport.   In a big binder, I have many US airport approach plates.   In a small binder, I carry the plates for airports I normally fly into, along with alternates.

I also carry an aircraft operating manual plus odds and ends such as a flashlight and spare eyeglasses.   Additionally, I carry my own headset which is handy if the cockpit speaker should fail or if I have a problem with my microphone.

6)   How does a person become a pilot?

There are two routes. One is to join the military. The first step is to be accepted to an Officer Training Program. After completing this program, the individual has to be qualified and selected to attend pilot training. At the completion of pilot training, which takes about one to two years, he or she will get wings. The new military pilot then goes to train on the aircraft of assignment. They will also undergo survival training.

The second route is civilian. It involves going to the local airport and earning a private pilot license. It cost me about $2,500 in 1980.   A student will learn about aerodynamics, aviation regulations,   airport   operations,   meteorology,   radio communications, navigation, and of course, how to operate the airplane. There is a written exam, oral exam and a flight test. This is the basic license and will allow you to rent or buy an airplane and take friends and relatives flying. If you want to fly for a living, you have a long way to go yet.

The next license is the Commercial Pilot. There's not much to learn, but the pilot has to demonstrate more experience and greater competency since this license will allow him or her to fly for hire. For the flight test, the airplane used will have retractable landing gear and flaps as well as a propeller which the pilot controls separately from the engine. The pilot will also take a written and oral exam.

A commercial pilot license, by itself, is good for sightseeing flights, towing banners or gliders and basically local area flying in good weather. To be fully useful, a pilot also needs an instrument rating. A private or commercial pilot may have it.

The instrument rating is like a license that allows a pilot to fly in bad weather. It is required when a flight is conducted without reference to the ground. This occurs when flying in or above clouds, through rain or snow showers, or fog or other obstruction to visibility. Instrument flying means flying solely by reference to instruments in the cockpit and navigating by electronic guidance. Normally, if a person wants to fly professionally, he or she will undergo commercial and instrument training at the same time. It cost me about $5,000 in the early 1980s. The instrument rating requires a written exam as well as the oral exam and flight test.

The next license is normally the Flight Instructor's License. This involves doing commercial pilot maneuvers from the right seat, and it took a few hours of practice before I could do a good landing again. When applying for this license, the applicant has to demonstrate the ability to *teach* how to fly an airplane. This license cost me less than $1,200 in 1985. This also requires written, oral, and flight tests.

The new instructor pilot now finds a job instructing and builds up flight time. Flight time is a measure of experience, but has nothing to do with the flying ability of a pilot. A guy or gal with

1,000 hours might fly much better and competently than someone with 3,000 hours. A new flight instructor will probably have about 200 to 250 hours. He will need at least 1,200 to 1,500 hours before anyone will consider him for employment in larger airplanes.

At some point, the pilot will have to get a multi-engine rating. As the name implies, it will allow him or her to fly an airplane with more than one engine. The main focus of the training is what to do if one engine fails. A multi-engine airplane also has more systems and is more complex than most single engine airplanes. The multi-engine airplane is usually faster and requires the pilot to be on the ball, more so than most single engine airplanes. This license cost me about $1,500 in 1983.

Another license to get is an add-on to the Flight Instructor's. It's called Instrument Instructor. This allows the instructor to teach students how to fly with reference to instruments only. His students will be in training for their instrument rating. This license cost me only a few hundred dollars.

Every license or rating involves flying with an official of the FAA (Federal Aviation Administration) or an FAA designated flight examiner. The flight test is preceded by an oral exam which may last from one to two hours. With the exception of the multi-engine rating, all licenses and ratings require a written exam, and 80% or better is passing.

Once enough time is accumulated, he or she may be hired to fly larger airplanes. My first airline job after instructing was flying a 15 passenger turbo-prop. It was a big step from what I had been doing, but it took me only a few hours of flying to get comfortable with it.

Since then, I have moved into a bigger, faster, and more complicated aircraft. It is more modern than many jets and uses TV screens instead of mechanical instruments. Ground school lasted two weeks. I spent seven days in a full motion simulator and two days training in the actual airplane. There were written and oral exams. The flight test is crucial. At most airlines, if you fail the first time, you will get a second try. If you fail again, you will likely be out of a job.

In summary, the licenses a pilot gets are: Private, Commercial, Instrument, Flight Instructor, Multi-engine, and Flight Instructor Instrument. At today's prices, it would probably run in the neighborhood of $15,000, but don't hold me to that.

Not to be left out is the Airline Transport Pilot license. It's like the Ph.D. of aviation. This license is required to act as a Captain at an airline or as the Pilot in Command of large aircraft and jets. It is earned on the basis of experience, a written test, and a flight test -- usually in a multi-engine airplane.

7)   How much control do pilots have over the actual departure and arrival times?

I would have to say, very little. We are always at the mercy of Air Traffic Control (ATC), weather, late passengers, late bags, late service from cleaners, catering, fueling, and lavatory personnel. If the company says to wait for some more bags, we wait. If ATC tells us we can expect to taxi 30 minutes late, so it goes.

The only thing we can do is make sure we are not the cause of the delay. We can try to make up time by asking ATC for more direct routing. We might be willing to tolerate a little turbulence to get a better tailwind or reduce the effects of a headwind. Other than that, we are merely spectators.

8)   How do pilots get their work schedule?

Every pilot receives a seniority number when he or she is hired. The number is very important as it will dictate what a pilot flies, where he or she is based, the schedule, position (Captain or Co-pilot) and indirectly, salary.

At the beginning of the month, an airline publishes the schedules for the following month. Each schedule is called a *line* (see figure A) and there could be over 100 just for co-pilots of a particular airplane type (say a Boeing 727) at a particular base (say Atlanta). The number one co-pilot will have to make one choice, and he will get it. The guy at the bottom of the list will get what's left. I happen to be number 11 out of 65. I make 11 choices and expect to get one of my top 4 picks.

When a pilot reviews the schedules, many factors will be considered. Some factors are: the report time, the ending time, number of days off, the specific days off, estimated overtime, amount of flying, and where the overnights are. Pilots who commute to work are usually interested in a schedule that allows them to commute (fly) to their base the day they start work. No one wants to commute on their day off and spend the night. They also want to finish in time to catch a flight back home.

Some pilots want weekends off. Others want overtime pay. Everyone is different. The pilots will enter their *bids* into a computer. A few days later, the results are published. At this point, the pilot knows when he is off and what cities he will be overnighting in. He also knows who the other crew members will be.

The schedule is made up of *pairings* (See Figure B). A pairing might be a one day trip or a four day trip. Each pairing has a number on the schedule. When the pilot sees that on November 14th he starts pairing number 001 (actually 7001), he can look up the pairing in a booklet. When he finds it, he will see every flight he has to do. It shows departure date/time/city, arrival date/time/city, flight number, pay value, and hotel information.

Figure A

```
LINE 28  CR.    82.08     31  1  2  3  4: 5  6: 7  8  9 10 11:12 13:14 15 16 17 18:19 20:21 22 23 24 25:
         TAFB  110.22     MO TU WE TH FR:SA SU:MO TU WE TH FR:SA SU:MO TU WE TH FR:SA SU:MO TU WE TH FR:
         BLK    82.08             020020020020            020020020                           020020020020
OFF  17  NO. DP'S 14      *  *  *  * EWREWREWREWR *  *  *  * EWREWREWR  *  *  *  * EWREWREWR  *  * EWR
         C/O     .00      020=1355/2148/0552,

LINE 29  CR.    82.08     31  1  2  3  4: 5  6: 7  8  9 10 11:12 13:14 15 16 17 18:19 20:21 22 23 24 25:
         TAFB  110.22     MO TU WE TH FR:SA SU:MO TU WE TH FR:SA SU:MO TU WE TH FR:SA SU:MO TU WE TH FR:
         BLK    82.08           020020020         020020020                 020020020
OFF  17  NO. DP'S 14      * EWREWREWR *: *  *: * EWREWREWR *: *  *: * EWREWREWR *: *  * EWREWREWR *:
         C/O     .00      020=1355/2148/0552,

LINE 30  CR.    81.21     31  1  2  3  4: 5  6: 7  8  9 10 11:12 13:14 15 16 17 18:19 20:21 22 23 24 25:
         TAFB  266.05     MO TU WE TH FR:SA SU:MO TU WE TH FR:SA SU:MO TU WE TH FR:SA SU:MO TU WE TH FR:
         BLK    81.21     014            :025                :001                :101
OFF  17  NO. DP'S 14      RSWORDEWR *  *: *  *:RSWIAHAUSEWR *: *  *: *:FLLCLEEWR *: *: *:RSWIAHAUSEWR *:
         C/O     .00      014=0930/1908/1533, 025=1500/2146/2554, 001=0530/1544/1805, 101=1500/1427/2209

LINE 31  CR.    81.02     31  1  2  3  4: 5  6: 7  8  9 10 11:12 13:14 15 16 17 18:19 20:21 22 23 24 25:
         TAFB  261.40     MO TU WE TH FR:SA SU:MO TU WE TH FR:SA SU:MO TU WE TH FR:SA SU:MO TU WE TH FR:
         BLK    81.02              :035                :025                           :035
OFF  17  NO. DP'S 14      *  *  *  *:FLLIAHEWR *  *  *  *:RSWIAHAUSEWR *  *  *  *:FLLIAHEWR *  *  *  *:
         C/O     .00      035=1930/2334/1457, 025=1500/2146/2554,
```

10

Figure B

```
BASE: ----> EWR  OCTOBER 31-NOVEMBER 30, 1994 727 PILOT PAIRINGS
DAY     FLT  CITY   ---> CKIN  BLK  GRND  BLK  PILOT  F/A      LAYOVER
  OA DH      PAIR   DEPT ARVL              TTL  DUTY  DUTY MEAL    /TYPE
-------------------------------------------------------------------------
E7001  EXCPT FR SA SU   ***OCT 31 ONLY***
  PILOT -->  0530    F/A -->  0530
 1 727   330 EWR BOS 0630 0737  1:07 0:53
 1 727   331 BOS EWR 0830 0954  1:24 0:41
 1 727       EWR FLL 1035 1327  2:52            5:23  8:12  8:12      19:13   S1
 ▬▬▬▬▬▬▬▬▬                                     ▬▬▬▬▬▬▬▬▬▬▬▬▬
  PILOT -->  0810    F/A -->  0755
 2 727  1165 FLL TPA 0840 0935  0:55 0:30
 2 727      *TPA IAH 1005 1114  2:09 1:56
 2 727   282 IAH CLE 1310 1642  2:32            5:36  8:47  9:02      14:08   S2
  SEE HOTEL LIST                                000-000-0000 ▬▬▬▬
  PILOT -->  0620    F/A -->  0605
 3 727   762 CLE EWR 0650 0814  1:24 0:51
 3 727       EWR SRQ 0905 1203  2:58 0:42
 3 727   763*SRQ EWR 1245 1529  2:44            7:06  9:24  9:39 SNK
                              TOTAL BLK:  18:05           TAFB:  58:14
- - - - - - - - - - - - - - - - - - - - - - - - - - - - - - - - - - - - -
(E7001) EXCPT FR SA SU     NOV 01-NOV 30              EXCEPT NOV 23 NOV 24
  PILOT -->  0530    F/A -->  0530
 1 727   330 EWR BOS 0630 0737  1:07 0:53
 1 727   331 BOS EWR 0830 0954  1:24 0:41
 1 727       EWR FLL 1035 1327  2:52            5:23  8:12  8:12      19:13   S1
 ▬▬▬▬▬▬▬▬▬                                     ▬▬▬▬▬▬▬▬▬▬▬▬▬
  PILOT -->  0810    F/A -->  0755
 2 727  1165 FLL TPA 0840 0935  0:55 0:30
 2 727      *TPA IAH 1005 1114  2:09 1:56
 2 727   282 IAH CLE 1310 1642  2:32            5:36  8:47  9:02      14:08   S2
  SEE HOTEL LIST                                000-000-0000 ▬▬▬▬
  PILOT -->  0620    F/A -->  0605
 3 727   762 CLE EWR 0650 0814  1:24 0:51
 3 727       EWR SRQ 0905 1203  2:58 0:42
 3 727   763*SRQ EWR 1245 1529  2:44            7:06  9:24  9:39 SNK
                              TOTAL BLK:  18:05           TAFB:  58:14
-------------------------------------------------------------------------
E7002  FR                  NOV 04-NOV 18
  PILOT -->  0530    F/A -->  0530
FR 727   330 EWR BOS 0630 0737  1:07 0:53
FR 727   331 BOS EWR 0830 0954  1:24 0:41
FR 727       EWR FLL 1035 1327  2:52            5:23  8:12  8:12      19:13   S1
         ▬▬▬▬▬▬▬▬▬                             ▬▬▬▬▬▬▬▬▬▬▬▬▬
  PILOT -->  0810    F/A -->  0755
SA 727  1165 FLL TPA 0840 0935  0:55 0:30
SA 727       TPA IAH 1005 1114  2:09            3:04  4:19  4:34      23:51   S1
  SEE HOTEL LIST                                000-000-0000 ▬▬▬▬
  PILOT -->  1035    F/A -->  1020
SU 727   492 IAH MIA 1105 1426  2:21            2:21  3:06  3:21      16:34   S1
         ▬▬▬▬▬▬▬▬▬▬                            ▬▬▬▬▬▬▬▬▬▬▬
         ▬▬▬▬▬▬▬▬▬▬
  PILOT -->  0630    F/A -->  0615
MO 727   294*MIA EWR 0700 0949  2:49 0:41                        SNK
MO 727   527 EWR DAB 1030 1300  2:30 0:30                        SNK
MO 727   384*DAB EWR 1330 1550  2:20            7:39  9:35  9:50
                              TOTAL BLK:  18:27           TAFB:  82:35
-------------------------------------------------------------------------
```

11

9)   How does a pilot land in the fog?

The most common approach is the Instrument Landing System
(ILS). Several components are involved, but most notable is an
antenna which gives course guidance to the runway and another
antenna which gives descent guidance to the landing end of the
runway. Initially, the pilot will be a few miles to the left or right
of the course. The air traffic controller will give the pilot a
heading in order to intersect and *join* the approach course.

The pilot at this point sees an instrument with a line going up and
down (vertical) on the left side (if he's to the right of course) and
another line going left to right (horizontal) on top. As the plane
approaches the course, the vertical line will begin to move
towards the center of the instrument. When it reaches the center,
the pilot is on course and lined up with the runway. He now
continues toward the runway, watching the horizontal line on top
of his instrument. As he approaches the glideslope (descent
guidance), the horizontal line will begin to move down towards
the center of the instrument. When it reaches the center, the pilot
is on the glideslope.

At this point, the instrument looks like it has a *plus* sign on it.
The pilot must keep both lines centered. He will begin a descent
in order to keep the horizontal line centered. The ILS usually
allows the pilot to descend to 200 feet above the ground. If the
pilot reaches this point and does not see at least the approach
lights at the end of the runway, he must execute a missed
approach (see question #47).

There are other approaches that are used; most do not provide
descent guidance. These are referred to as non-precision

approaches. The pilot still lines up with the runway, but descends to pre-determined altitudes at certain locations, normally measured in miles from the navigation station in use. At the end of the approach, the pilot will descend to a final altitude and start timing. When a calculated amount of time has elapsed, he must see the runway or execute the missed approach (see question #47).

10)   What sort of training does the airline give the pilot?

All pilots have either the Commercial or Airline Transport Pilot license when they are hired. Once hired by the airline, the pilot will receive training in the type airplane he will fly. Every airplane, especially those for airlines, is very different. A Boeing 747 pilot can't hop into a DC-10 and fly.

A new pilot, or one transferring from another airplane type, will first attend ground school which could last from two to six weeks. It's in ground school where the pilot learns about each system of the airplane, such as electrical and hydraulic. Pilots learn about voltage, pressures and temperatures in the system and when valves or electrical connections will open or close. There may be several oral and/or written exams during ground school.

Pilots have to know what they are doing when they turn a knob or flip a switch because it usually has some affect on another part of the system. It's definitely important to know the systems when something doesn't work properly. By the way, when something does fail, the pilots follow a checklist which is very specific about what to do (See Figure C).

Figure C

E. HYDRAULIC FAILURE (Continued)

2. Loss Of The Green System

The loss of hydraulic systems caused by the loss of mechanical and electric hydraulic pumps or by hydraulic fluid leakage is indicated by:

MAIN PUMP LOW PRESS and ELEC PUMP lights or LOW LEVEL light illuminated on the hydraulic panel.

INOP light illuminated, below 120 KIAS, on the rudder panel.

HYD and RUDDER (below 120 KIAS) lights illuminated on the MAP.

CAUTION light flashing.

Green Hydraulic Pressure . . . . CHECK

If hydraulic pressure normal, refer to LOSS of HYDRAULIC MAIN PUMP

Loss of Green Hydraulic pressure means loss of:
- Landing gear retraction and normal extension
- Nosewheel steering
- Outboard normal brakes
- Outboard flaps
- Green rudder power
- Forward Door Actuator

Green System Electric Hydraulic Pump · · · · · · · · · · OFF

Approach and landing configurations:
Gear; DOWN refer to ABNORMAL LANDING GEAR EXTENSION, FREEFALL.
Flaps; UP
Target Airspeed; 0 V_{REF} + 10 KIAS
Reference Airspeed; 0 V_{REF}
GPWS 1 C/B (J25) . . . . PULL
Do not attempt to taxi

14

When the pilot has successfully completed ground school, he may attend cockpit procedures training (CPT). It depends on the airline and airplane. The CPT uses a device which is just like the cockpit of the airplane except nothing works (some lights and instruments may simulate actual operation). Its purpose is for the pilot to learn the location of every switch, button, knob, light, and instrument. He will learn if the switch is pulled, pushed, turned, or a combination. Many switches have different shapes and sizes so the pilot can identify them by touch.

The final stage of training takes place in the simulator. The simulator, from outside, looks like a big, bumpy box on hydraulic lifts. Inside, it is a fully realistic cockpit with a very realistic view out the windows. Initially, the pilot will learn to fly the airplane. He will take-off, climb to whatever altitude the instructor desires, and do some airwork. This involves flying the airplane in ways not done with passengers on board. One such maneuver is the steep turn. It may be done as a complete turn in one direction using a bank of up to 60 degrees. Normal bank with passengers is about 15 to 20 degrees.

Once the pilot is comfortable flying the airplane (simulator), he will learn to deal with failures and emergencies. When the training is complete, he has to undergo an exam known as a *check-ride*. An airline examiner will be there, and there may also be an examiner from the Federal Aviation Administration. The pilot will have an oral exam and then fly the simulator.

It doesn't end there. Every six months, a Captain has to return to the simulator to remain proficient. A co-pilot does it every year. If they ever fail, they can be fired but will usually get a second chance. The same thing goes for the airplane systems. Just before a pilot returns to the simulator, he attends a short ground school to remain current on systems. We also attend training to learn how to work as a team -- commonly known as cockpit resource management.

Unlike most professions, a pilot's training never ends and neither does the testing. If we ever fail a simulator ride or medical exam, we can be abruptly terminated. If a pilot goes to another airline, he has to start at the bottom regardless of his experience. There is no such thing as job security for professional pilots.

11) Sometimes, while rolling down the runway, I hear and feel a lot of *thumps*. What causes it?

Many airports, especially large metropolitan airports, have lights mounted in the pavement of the runway. These lights are called centerline lights. They run from one end of the runway to the other and are useful to the pilot during periods of low visibility. As the plane rolls down the runway, the tires on the nose gear may ride over the small metal plate shielding the lights which causes a *thump*.

12) What do the letters and numbers on signs near the taxiway mean?

Like streets in your neighborhood, all taxiways have a name. Instead of using a word, airports use the letters of the alphabet. Pilots have taxi diagrams to use at the airport and, believe it or not, taxiing can be more difficult than flying, especially at night at an unfamiliar airport. The yellow signs help guide the pilot on his route to the runway or terminal as directed by the ground controller in the control tower. Runways have numbers orientated to their magnetic heading. Runway 32 would have a course very close to 320 degrees. Runway signs are red. If you see the letter

L, C, or R after the runway number, then there are parallel runways: 32L (left), 32C (center), and 32R (right).

13)   What do the different colored lights at the airport mean?

The following colors are common: green, red, white, and blue. Green lights identify the beginning of the landing portion of the runway, which is the threshold. On most runways, this happens to be at the beginning of the pavement. Green lights are also used along the center of taxiways, especially to lead a pilot off the runway after landing. Red lights are used to mark the end of the runway and obstructions. Blue lights mark the edges of taxiways. White lights are used for the edges of the runway. Some runways have lights mounted in the pavement, especially down the centerline.

As you move down the runway, you would see white lights on the edges and middle of the runway. When 3,000 feet of runway remains, the centerline lights become alternate red and white. At 2,000 feet, the edge lights are red and at 1,000 feet, all lights are red.

Many airports have a rotating beacon. From the air, these are seen as a green flash then a white flash. It can be seen long before the airport and is often a help in locating an airport surrounded by a city. Military airports have a green flash then two white flashes.

Airplanes have a red light on the left wingtip, a green light on the right wingtip and a white light mounted so as to be visible from behind. In flight, we can determine which way another airplane is moving based on which lights we see. We also follow the same *rules of the road* as ships. If an airplane is converging from my right, I will see his red (left wingtip) light and yield. He will see my green (right wingtip) light. Airplanes also have a flashing red light. It may be rotating or a strobe. It is normally on to indicate an operating aircraft. We also have white strobe lights to help us stand out in the night sky.

We usually turn on all the landing lights and taxi lights when cleared for take-off and leave them on until above 10,000 feet. That is to help other aircraft see us in the congested departure/arrival area.

14)   What are the little red and white shacks I see by the runway?

In bad weather (low visibility), pilots normally use the Instrument Landing System to navigate to the runway. Not every runway has this. There are two transmitters at the runway from which an instrument in the cockpit receives its information. One transmitter is in the red and white shack near the edge of the runway. This is where the pilot gets his glideslope, or descent, information from. It will guide him down to the landing end of the runway. At the opposite end of the runway is an antenna which gives the pilot *turn left or right* information to line up with the runway. This is not a shack but a contraption of bars. It looks like monkey bars at a playground.

While you're looking out the window, you might also notice a transmissometer. Near the edge of the runway are two platforms. On one, a device transmits light. The other platform receives the light. As visibility deteriorates, because of fog or heavy rain/snow, the amount of light received at the platform decreases. Based on the amount of light measured at the receiving end, a measurement known as Runway Visual Range (RVR) is made.

Basically, the air traffic controller informs the pilot of the RVR. It tells the pilot how many feet down the runway he can expect to see. When in use, the visibility is normally less than 5,000 feet.

Some airports also have a navigation station on the field. The most common one is a VOR (VHF omni-direction range). It is white and looks like an upside down ice cream cone on a saucer with a small shack underneath.

15)   What do the markings on the runway mean?

At the beginning of the runway, or threshold, are eight white stripes. Next is a number which identifies the particular runway and its approximate direction. When a plane is lined up on runway 18, its heading should be very close to 180 degrees, or South. Five hundred feet from the threshold markings is the touchdown zone, identified by six white stripes. Five hundred feet further are two solid white boxes painted on the pavement. These are the fixed distance markers and they identify the first (or last) thousand feet of runway. At 1,500 feet and 2,000 feet, there are 4 white stripes and then, continuing at 500 foot intervals, 2 white stripes until the markings reverse toward the opposite threshold (See Figures D1 and D2).

The threshold marks the beginning of the usable part of the runway for landing. There may be plenty of pavement before the threshold, but because of an obstruction or other reason, it's unsuitable for landing. That section of runway will have arrows pointing towards the threshold. It is still all right to begin a take-off from that area.

Figure D1 / D2

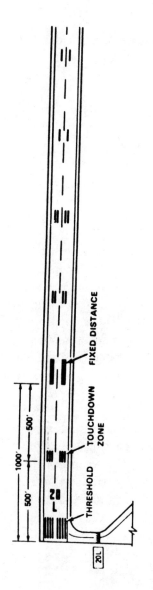

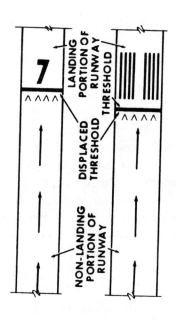

Source: Federal Aviation Administration

The fixed distance marking is the aiming point for the pilot of a landing aircraft. Again, it's located 1,000 feet from the threshold. Some runways don't have these markings, normally because they are not used with an Instrument Landing System.

As your plane moves from the taxiway onto the runway, it will cross four yellow lines. The first two are solid, and the next two are dashed. The pilot cannot cross the solid lines without permission of the controller since he is taxiing onto a runway. Exiting a runway means the pilot will cross the dashed lines first, and he then doesn't need permission to cross any lines.

16)   What makes a plane fly?

Lift. Many chapters have been written about it. I will explain it in its most basic concept -- no math formulas or aerodynamic language. You first need to understand one critical part: Bernoulli's principle. Daniel Bernoulli was an 18th Century Swiss physicist who used a venturi tube for demonstrations. A venturi tube is a hollow tube with a narrow throat. When fluid encounters the narrow throat, it accelerates and continues on. You do this when you put your thumb over the outlet of your garden hose to make the water travel far.

Here is the most technical part. The fluid contains X amount static pressure and Y amount kinetic energy. If the fluid increases its speed as it passes the venturi throat, then it has more kinetic energy than when it started; therefore, it gave up static pressure. That's because energy cannot be created or destroyed; it can only be changed. The fluid gave up pressure in order to accelerate. That's Bernoulli's principle (See Figure E).

Figure E

Static Pressure Decreases

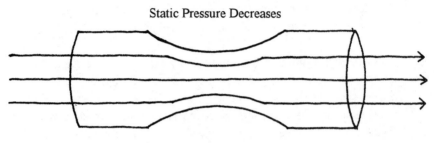

Kinetic Energy Increases

Drawings By John Cronin

Figure F

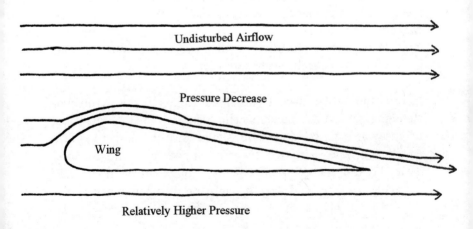

Undisturbed Airflow

Pressure Decrease

Wing

Relatively Higher Pressure

22

As an airplane accelerates down the runway, Bernoulli's principle begins to take effect (See Figure F). The wing acts as the narrow part of the venturi tube. Air encountering the wing will, just like in the venturi tube, give up pressure in order to accelerate. Air pressure above the wing is decreased, but the pressure below the wing is unaffected. The result is relatively higher pressure under the wing and that pushes the wing up . . . lift!

17) When approaching to land, the sound of the engines is always changing. Why?

The air traffic controller will sometimes restrict an airplane to a particular airspeed. Imagine flying into the destination area and the controller slows you down. Just like a car, you have to reduce the thrust of the engine. Pilots know that a particular power setting will result in a particular airspeed and will reduce power as required. If the controller instructs to slow down without delay, then the power may be substantially reduced to expedite the speed reduction. When the aircraft reaches the desired airspeed, the power will have to be increased to maintain it.

If the aircraft is cleared to a lower altitude, the power will have to be reduced. Again, like a car, if you are cruising steady at 55 MPH and then start going downhill, your speed will increase unless you reduce power. Every time the pilot changes altitude, he will have to change the power setting to maintain the assigned airspeed.

Changes in wind direction and velocity will also affect airspeed (and groundspeed) so a pilot may find himself *milking* the power levers to maintain a particular airspeed and descent rate during the approach to landing.

18)   Do airplanes fly if some parts or systems are broken?

Yes. Airplanes have what is called a *Minimum Equipment List*.
If an item does not work, the MEL will indicate if the part or
system is required for flight and under what conditions the
airplane can fly without it (See Figure G).

If a back-up fuel pump does not work, the MEL may say you can
fly as long as all other pumps are working and one pump is
operated continuously. If the weather radar does not work, the
MEL may say you can fly only if thunderstorms can be visually
avoided. Some parts must work and the MEL will not allow
flight without them. Depending on the part or system, the MEL
may state a limiting number of days or flights before the part
must be repaired or replaced (which is actually known as a
Deferred Maintenance Item).

19)   How can I improve my chances for survival in an
       airplane accident?

Pay attention to the flight attendant's (or pilot's) safety briefing or,
on some aircraft, the video presentation. Review the safety
briefing card. If you don't understand something, ask the flight
attendant. Many airliners today have isle path lighting. These
lights lead to exits. They are activated either manually by the
crew or automatically by the electrical system. As a back-up to
these lights, you should know how many rows to crawl to reach
the exits behind you and in front of you.

Figure G

███████████		MINIMUM EQUIPMENT LIST			
SYSTEM: 28 FUEL		PERFORMANCE PENALTY		FROM: MMEL REV. 5 6-24-93	
NORMAL COMPLEMENT OF EQUIPMENT		MINIMUM EQUIPMENT REQUIRED FOR DEPARTURE		ADVANCE NOTIFICATION TO DISPATCH REQUIRED	
	CATEGORY				
-21-1 Ejector Main Fuel Pumps	C	2	0	(O) May be inoperative provided: a) Two electric pumps in associated tank operate normally, b) One electric pump in associated tank remains on during operation, and c) AFM limitations are complied with.	YES
-21-2 Electric Fuel Boost Pumps					
1) 2 Pump Installation					
2) 4 Pump Installation	C	4	2	One pump per tank may be inoperative provided remaining pumps operate normally.	
-21-3 Motive Flow Shutoff Valves	C	2	0	(M)(O) May be inoperative provided: a) Valve(s) is secured CLOSED, b) Two electric pumps in associated tank operate normally, c) One electric pump in associated tank remains on during operation, and d) AFM limitations are complied with.	
-22-1 Pressure Refueling System	C	1	0		
1) Auto Mode	C	1	0	May be inoperative provided: a) manual mode operates normally, and b) Vent valves are verified open.	
2) Manual Mode	C	1	0		

Sitting next to an emergency exit is a responsibility not to be taken lightly. People's lives will depend on your actions. You should be thoroughly knowledgeable in the operation of the exit and when it should be used. On some aircraft, for example, certain exits should not be opened after a water landing; you could flood the cabin. The safety briefing card explains this. If anything happens during a flight, follow the directions of the crew. If you are uncomfortable, ask to be seated somewhere else. By the way, if you like a lot of leg room, you will enjoy the exit row seats. They are usually wider to allow people to exit (be advised that you may not be able to recline your seat). If you sit in an isle seat, be on guard everytime the overhead bin is opened. If you're not alert, a fellow passenger may open the bin and a briefcase or bag will fall on your head.

Wear comfortable shoes with laces or some sort of fastening device. If you wear sandals or high heels, you will probably lose them during impact or evacuation. You then have to go barefoot through the wreckage which will be littered with hot, twisted and sharp pieces of metal, plastic, and glass. Wear pants. They provide better protection than shorts or a skirt. I cannot tell you the tail section is safer than the front or an isle seat is better than a window seat. Every accident and airplane presents a unique situation. Fortunately, accidents are very rare. On a final note, you should be sober and drug free. You will likely have a tough time evacuating an aircraft if you are under the influence of alcohol or drugs. In case you didn't know, an airline cannot board a passenger who appears to be incapacitated (drunk or high).

20)   What is a go-around?

A go-around is an aborted approach to landing. It can happen if the pilot determines the aircraft is not properly configured to land (maybe all the landing gear didn't extend), or on a proper approach path (too high). The airplane may encounter a severe windshear or turbulence from the preceding aircraft. A go-around may be initiated by the air traffic controller or pilot. If the controller sees that the preceding landing aircraft cannot get off the runway fast enough, he will issue the go-around instruction. Basically, the go-around is conducted when it is not safe to continue the approach or land.

A go-around is started by applying a predetermined amount of power. Based on temperature and field elevation, the pilot might apply from 90% to 100% power. The flaps are usually brought to a take-off setting and the landing gear retracted. Every situation and airplane is different, so the procedure varies. Once the airplane is climbing out of the area, the pilot will be placed back in the approach sequence or, depending on the situation, diverted to another airport or holding pattern.

21)   Why do the plane's engines get loud during landing?

Upon landing, the pilot will apply reverse thrust if necessary, which is most of the time. Reverse thrust is most effective while the plane is going fast. As the airplane slows down, reverse thrust is reduced or discontinued and normal tire braking (like a car) is used. On a jet engine, reverse thrust is attained by redirecting the exhaust gases forward. On some Boeing 737s, you may see the sides of the engine open up. The ends of both sides will meet to block the exhaust and direct it forward. On other airplanes, you will notice the rear half of the engine (actually an outer casing) move rearward. Again, the normal exhaust is being blocked and redirected forward.

At the same time, the engine thrust will increase to a level determined by the engine manufacturer. So the increased noise comes from an increase in engine thrust and the deflecting of the exhaust.

In the case of a propeller driven airplane, the blade angle of the propeller will go to a setting where, instead of pushing air rearward, it now pushes air forward. The engine, like the jet, will also increase thrust. Not all propeller airplanes have reverse thrust.

22)   What are the strips of metal that come up out of the wing during landing?

They are known as speed brakes or spoilers. When the plane lands, the pilot wants to get the airplane's weight on the landing gear. That will allow for better braking and control. By raising spoilers, the pilot disrupts the flow of air over the wing and destroys much of the lift. Without lift, the wing cannot support the weight of the aircraft. The spoilers also create drag and help to slow the airplane. You may observe these devices deploy during flight. Don't worry; it means the pilot is going to descend very rapidly. Without getting into aerodynamics, I will give a basic idea of how they work.

Let's say the airplane is moving at an airspeed of 270 knots and descending at 2,000 feet per minute. The air traffic controller may, for some reason, need the pilot to expedite the descent. When the pilot extends the spoilers (or speed brakes), he creates drag and disrupts lift. The pilot can either maintain the descent rate and give up (reduce) airspeed, or maintain the airspeed and descend at a faster rate.

Sometimes a plane may be reduced to a slow airspeed and then instructed to descend. If the pilot finds that the descent will require an increase in airspeed, he will use the spoilers. That way, he can maintain the assigned airspeed and still perform a descent.

23)   How does a jet engine work?

There are three words to explain this: suck, squeeze, and blow. There are three parts to a jet engine (See Figure H). The first part is the intake and compression. This is where the outside air is drawn in and compressed. The compressor has a circular shape with many blades. You can see it at the front of the engine. There may be several of them. These compressors are driven, through a shaft, by turbines in the exhaust section.

Compressing air makes it very hot. The next part is combustion. Fuel is mixed with the hot compressed air and ignited in the combustion chamber. Once the fuel is ignited during engine start, it burns continuously. That's to say, there is always a fire in the engine.

This process further heats the air.   In the plane I fly, the temperature during cruise flight is about 550 degrees Celsius. That's over 1,000 degrees Fahrenheit. It can reach 680 degrees Celsius at low altitudes. This hot air exits with great force and basically pushes the airplane forward. As the air is exhausted, it passes turbines, which are like windmills. These turbines are connected to the compressors at the front of the engine by a shaft. The turbines' job is to keep the compressors turning.

In summary, you can think of it as two windmills connected at their centers by a shaft. One turns the other. By the way, as the pilot moves the power levers, he is changing the amount of fuel being fed to the fire and that changes the temperature and overall engine thrust.

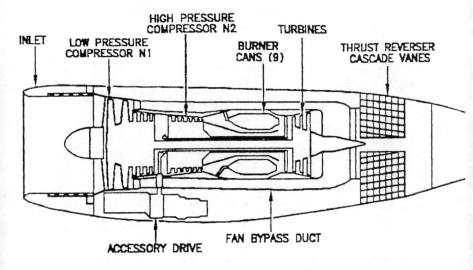

BASIC JT8D TURBOFAN ENGINE

Figure H

24)   Why are there different types of airplanes?

First of all, there is competition between manufacturers. Boeing might build a twin engine jet for short flights, and Douglas will put out a competitive version. Generally, a plane is designed for a certain market. There is the short haul market which involves frequent flights of short duration. An airline might run a flight between New York and Boston every hour like a bus. Because the flights are so frequent, there is not much time for many passengers to gather. The result is that flights depart frequently with less than 200 passengers. For this type of flying, the airline needs a small jet. The Boeing 737 series is popular as is the DC-9 or MD80. Some airlines have small commuter jets built by Fokker.

At the other end of the spectrum, is the world of international, overseas flying. These flights take many hours and require a lot of fuel. An airline might operate two or three flights a day. A large number of passengers can accumulate so the airplane will have to be large. A Boeing 747 can carry over 500 passengers. Because of the length of flights (in time), the passengers will need meals and entertainment (movies).

Once again, planes are built for a particular job and each manufacturer produces its own version of the ideal aircraft. An airline looking to buy an airplane will look at price, how much money per seat mile it will cost to operate, mechanical reliability, and ease of carrying out maintenance. Availability of parts and manufacturer support are also important.

25)   Why do planes fly so high?

For one thing, jet engines are much more fuel efficient at high altitudes where the air is less dense. The fuel consumed at 7,000 feet will be significantly greater than at 34,000 feet. Another reason is to be above the weather. Most weather (rain, snow, clouds) occurs at altitudes within 15,000 feet of the earth's surface. By flying high, you will usually be in clear air and away from turbulence. One more reason is to take advantage of the jet stream when heading Easterly. The jet stream is sort of like a raging river of air high in the sky.

26)   Why do the engines get quieter right after take-off?

The amount of power required for take-off is computed before the flight. If a plane requires less than 100% power (thrust), then the pilots will use the reduced power setting and save a little wear and tear on the engines. In an emergency, a pilot can always push the power levers as far as they will go. The engines might have to be replaced afterwards, but they can produce enormous thrust for a short period of time if necessary.

Once the airplane is safely airborne, the power will be reduced to an initial climb power setting. Not only is this good for the engines, but it reduces noise to the communities below.

27)   What are all those tiny pieces of metal sticking out of the wing?

They are commonly referred to as *vortex generators*. A vortex from an airplane looks like a sideways tornado. You may see vortex generators on top of the wing or on the side of the tail. As the name implies, they generate (create) a vortex. They are used to prevent the air from separating from the wing or other surface area. They also aid in the effectiveness of controls.

By controls I mean the ailerons (tiny flap-like devices near the wingtips used to raise and lower a wing) or rudder (the moving part of the tail; it travels to the left and right). You will commonly see vortex generators just ahead of the ailerons. You might get to see a vortex trailing off the wingtip during damp or misty days (See Figures I1-4).

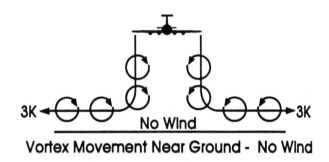

Vortex Movement Near Ground - No Wind

Source: Federal Aviation Administration

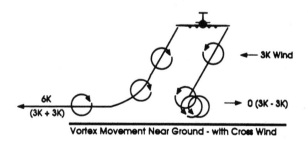

Vortex Movement Near Ground - with Cross Wind

Figure I1 / I2

Figure I3 / I4

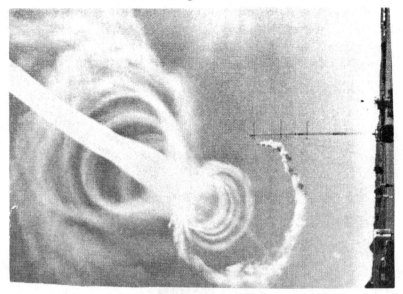

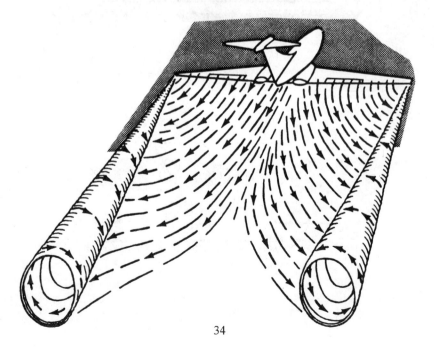

Source: Federal Aviation Administration

34

28)   What are the little pieces of wire hanging off the back of the wing?

You may sometimes notice as many as five short stubby wires sticking out from the back of a wingtip. You may also notice them on the tail. They are *static wicks*. As a plane flies through fine dust or moisture, it develops a static charge. The static wicks are a means for this *static electricity* to discharge. In a more dramatic circumstance, you will see St. Elmo's fire. It is harmless. It is simply a luminous glow caused by the static discharge. On a pilot's windshield, it can appear as webs of electricity, dancing and flickering like little lightning bolts.

29)   What does the tail do?

The *little wing* is referred to as a horizontal stabilizer. It is much like a wing except it produces lift on the bottom, that is, towards the ground. In effect, it's an upside down wing. This causes the rear of the airplane to be pushed towards the ground. It's done to balance the airplane since the front end is pulled down by gravity. The plane is like a see-saw, and the plane pivots on the wings.

Mounted to the horizontal stabilizer is the elevator. The elevator is controlled by the pilot pulling or pushing on the control wheel in the cockpit. It controls the airplane's *pitch*, which is the up and down motion of the nose.

The part of the tail sticking up is the vertical stabilizer. The rudder is attached to it. By pushing the rudder pedals (at the pilot's feet), the pilot moves the rudder left and right. This in turn makes the nose go left and right. The rudder helps to turn the plane.

In a nutshell, a plane turns when the pilot banks the aircraft. In level flight, the lift from the wings pushes the plane up. If the wings are banked, the lift is also being banked. The lift will push the plane into a turn. The pilot will have to use rudder so the tail follows the plane through the turn. If, in a left turn, the pilot did not use enough rudder, you would feel yourself slouching to your left. If the pilot used too much rudder, you would feel yourself slouching to the right. The first example is called a *slip*. The second example is a *skid*. If everything is perfect, you will feel like gravity is holding you naturally in the seat, no matter how steeply the plane banks.

30)   What is a turbo-prop aircraft?

A turbo-prop airplane is powered by a jet engine but receives thrust from a propeller. Basically, one or more turbines (like windmills) are placed in the exhaust section of the engine. They are on a shaft that is connected to the propeller. Because the turbine turns rapidly, there are reduction gears so that, on my airplane for example, a turbine turning at 19,530 RPM (revolutions per minute) makes the propeller turn at 1,302 RPM.

You may notice a pilot turn the propeller by hand or see it blow around in the wind. The propeller is not connected to anything other than reduction gears and the turbines in the exhaust section.

31)   How is cabin temperature controlled?

If you already read how a jet engine works, then you know the front part, the compressors, compress the air to make it hot. Some of this air is directed to *packs* and is called *bleed air*. The system varies from airplane to airplane, but here is the basic operation:

Some of the hot air (bleed air) continues through plumbing to a mixing chamber. The rest of the hot air goes to an air cycle machine (ACM). In this ACM, the hot air drives an expansion turbine and later enters the turbine. The expansion turbine causes the air to become cold, which is the opposite of what a compressor does. This very cold air meets the hot *bleed air* at the mixing chamber. A valve there regulates the mixture so as to arrive at the desired temperature. It is then directed to either floor vents or ceiling vents.

32)   How are planes pressurized?

I don't think any plane is perfectly sealed. You are not sealed in and kept at whatever altitude the airport happens to be at. The pressurized air comes from the compressors in the jet engine. A valve in the fuselage (body) of the airplane opens a certain amount to keep the cabin at the desired pressure.

Airplanes can keep sea level air pressure in the cabin up to a certain altitude. In my airplane, we can maintain sea level up to about 17,000 feet. After that, the cabin altitude must increase. At 32,000 feet, the pressure in the cabin is equal to 8,000 feet.

Before take-off, the pilots will set an instrument to the cruising altitude they plan to fly at. The instrument tells them what altitude the cabin will be at. After take-off, the system will allow air to slowly leak out of the airplane until the cabin is at the set altitude. When they begin to descend for landing at the destination, the pressurization instrument is set to the elevation of the airport. The system will allow air pressure in the cabin to increase until it is equal to your destination. If this isn't done properly (maybe the system isn't working right), one of two things might happen. You land, open the door, and air will rush in or out.

In summary, pressurizing an airplane is like blowing into a balloon. The compressors pump in air but a valve acts as a controlled leak to maintain the desired pressure.

33)   Why does the plane taxi out with only one engine running?

In a propeller driven airplane, it is very obvious that a single engine taxi is being performed. If the propeller is stationary or just blowing in the wind, the engine is probably not running. I say probably because some airplanes have a *prop brake*. It allows for the engine to run, and thus supply electricity and temperature controlled air, without the danger of a turning propeller.

If the pilot knows it will take a long time to taxi, he may elect to start only one or two engines. This will save fuel. Jet aircraft also taxi out on one or two engines; you just don't know it. Some airports require a long distance to travel from the ramp to the runway. Sometimes, there may be up to 40 airplanes ahead of you and it can take over one hour before you take-off (been to Newark lately?). It just doesn't make sense to burn fuel unless there are other operational factors to consider.

34)   What are the flaps for?

Flaps change the shape of the wing and may also increase the total surface area of the wing. The result is an increase in lift which allows the pilot to fly at a low airspeed. For landing, the

38

pilot can slow down and make a steep approach using flaps. Without flaps, he would have to approach at a much faster speed and may not have enough runway for the landing. For take-off, the pilot wants a lot of lift in order to use a minimum amount of runway.

When the flaps are lowered, as for landing, they also increase drag. The airplane will slow down but eventually the pilot will have to increase power (thrust) to overcome the drag and maintain the slower airspeed. This is why you may sometimes notice a change in the sound of the engines shortly after the flaps are adjusted, especially during the approach to landing.

35)   What are the moving parts on front of the wing for?

There are several devices: slots, slates or leading edge flaps. Like flaps, these also change the shape of the wing to increase lift. Sometimes, the airplane is flying into the air in a manner that causes air to come at the plane from below. Watch a jet coming in to land. It is pointed towards the sky, like a take-off, but the airplane is descending to land. As far as the wing is concerned, air is coming at it from below and not head on.

The difference between air hitting the wing head on or below is known as the *angle of attack*. On airplanes, the angle of attack could be so great as to disturb the smooth flow of air above the wing. The result is, turbulent air and a loss of lift. To prevent this, some airplanes have a slot.

A slot, when used, results in an opening between the front of the wing and the wing itself. Air comes up from under the wing and is guided through the opening, the slot. It then continues smoothly over the wing.

A leading edge flap acts as a scoop. There is no opening. The flap often folds down from the front of the wing to cause a large curved area to form. When in use, it will direct air to the top of the wing during high angles of attack, such as during take-off and approach to landing.

36)   What is an aborted take-off?

It occurs anytime the pilot stops the take-off after a take-off clearance has been received from the control tower. During the take-off, the pilot flying steers the plane down the runway. The other pilot will monitor the engine instruments to make sure they are operating normally. If any indication is outside limits or just not normal, the take-off may be aborted. We are trained so that the illumination of any warning light or activation of an oral warning system will result in an immediate abort. The philosophy is that there is no time to see what is wrong so we should just abort and then figure it out.

An aborted take-off can be risky. Before the flight, pilots figure out an airspeed known as V_1. This is the go/no go speed. Once this airspeed is reached during the take-off, the pilots are committed to flight. If an airplane is just about to reach V_1 and an abort is initiated, the pilot will probably use maximum braking. Every situation is different. The use of maximum brakes can cause the tires of the landing gear to blow out and possibly result in fire at that location.

Normally, aborted take-offs aren't that dramatic. You will feel the airplane accelerating and then, when the abort is initiated, the engines go to reverse (which is noisy), then speed brakes come up out of the wing and the pilot applies brakes to the tires. It's no big deal except for the paperwork. That's another story.

37)   Is lightning dangerous?

Not really. It's the storm producing the lightning that can be dangerous. Airplanes are designed and built with lightning strikes taken into consideration. A bolt of lightning normally passes through the aircraft harmlessly. It may enter at the nose and exit off a wingtip or the tail (See Figure J). Many times, the lightning leaves behind a pinhole-sized mark and scorches the area where it struck. Sometimes, however, it might cause a larger hole. If the damage is great enough, the strong airflow may tear a piece off the aircraft. The aircraft will be inspected by maintenance upon landing. There is no record of an inflight explosion due to a lightning strike igniting fuel, not that I know of anyway.

The storm that produces lightning is dangerous because it contains just about every hazard known to aviation. These hazards include: torrential rain, hail, icing, and powerful updrafts and downdrafts along with rapid and extreme changes in wind speed and direction (See Figure K).

Pilots want to see their families again as much as you do, so we do not normally fly into these storms on purpose. There are several levels of storm intensities, however, and we may fly near one or weave around several. There may be turbulence in the area around the storm.

Lightning, as well as the storm itself, often seems closer than it really is. From your point of view, a storm may appear to be only several miles away when, in reality, it could be 150 miles away. I always need the weather radar to tell me the distance to the storm; it's impossible to guess.

Figure J

LIGHTNING STRIKE ZONES

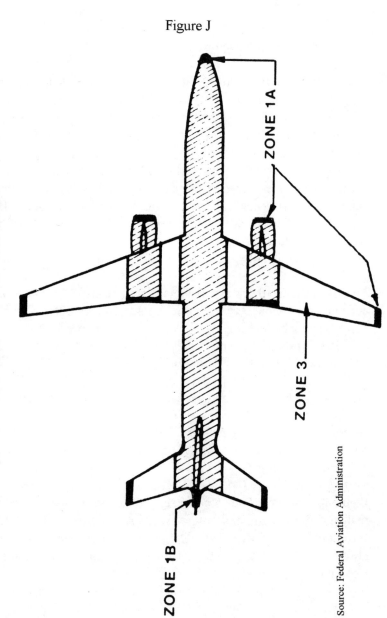

ZONE 1A

ZONE 3

ZONE 1B

Source: Federal Aviation Administration

42

38)   What is weather radar?

It is a device which, like many types of radar, sends out a signal and processes that signal if it returns. If there is nothing for the radar signal to hit, it cannot be reflected to the aircraft and the radar screen will be blank. A thunderstorm contains large amounts of water in various states (liquid, gas, and solid). When a radar signal encounters this precipitation, it is reflected back to the aircraft and processed. Based upon the amount of time it takes the signal to return, the weather radar can determine the distance to the storm. The radar can also determine the intensity of the storm by how strong the signal is when it returns. A storm can be so strong that much of the signal is absorbed. The result is that a shadow appears on the radar. To the untrained eye, it would appear to be the best place to go since there is no image.

A trained pilot will recognize this *clear* area as a shadow and avoid that region. The purpose of weather radar is to avoid storm penetration.

39)   What is turbulence? Will it break the wings?

One form of turbulence is caused by convection and is most common at lower altitudes. It is caused by the sun's heating of the ground. Some areas, like a parking lot, reflect heat back into the atmosphere. As this hot air rises, it cools and eventually sinks. Basically, this sort of turbulence is caused by columns of rising and sinking air. To avoid this during the summer on commuter aircraft, consider early morning flights.

Another form of turbulence occurs in clouds. The most common *bumpy* cloud is the cumulus cloud. It is the big fluffy type you see on a summer afternoon. The cloud is like a sign-post that tells the pilot that the air is unstable. Warm air can hold more moisture than colder air. As the warm moist air rises, it cools and the moisture is *squeezed* out, becoming a visible cloud. You will have turbulence in this cloud because the air is in constant motion, mostly rising and sinking.

Turbulence is also experienced on windy, gusty days. Just like water in a river swirls around obstacles, so does air when it encounters mountains or buildings. Because the airflow is disturbed, it moves from different directions at different speeds. The result is the airplane encounters constantly changing winds.

The wings of the airplane are designed to flex. Depending on the aircraft, the flexing might be hard to notice or more obvious than you'd like. Some wings flex several feet.

A little turbulence is not a problem, but if it's severe and/or continuous, the pilot will slow the airplane to a turbulence penetration speed. This speed is provided by the aircraft manufacturer. At or below this speed, the aircraft wing will stall before it breaks. In a nutshell, if a column of air rises with enough force, the flow of air over the wing will be disturbed resulting in a loss of lift (momentarily). This is far better than breaking the wing. The slower airspeed will also provide a better ride, just as if you were driving on a bumpy road. If you think turbulence will make you sick, consider a seat in the center of the airplane; avoid the rear seats.

40)   What is windshear? Is it dangerous?

Windshear is a sudden change in wind direction and/or velocity.
An example of windshear can be found during thunderstorm
activity. Very cold air from the thunderstorm descends rapidly.
When it encounters the ground, it spreads out in all directions.
You may have experienced this *gust* as a storm approached.
While this is happening, the storm is drawing air into itself. This
air may be only a few hundred feet above the ground. The result
is a surface wind moving away from the storm and a wind aloft
moving toward the storm (See Figure K).

It is most dangerous to airplanes during the most critical phases
of flight: take-offs and landings. During these times, the airplane
is flying slowly and is close to the ground. Let us say an airplane
can't fly at a speed of less than 120 MPH (miles per hour). Let us
also say it is approaching to land and is flying at 140 MPH. If a
10 MPH headwind suddenly shifts into a 10 MPH tailwind
(windshear), the airplane's speed will instantly go from 140 MPH
to 120 MPH and may cause the airplane to sink and contact the
ground prematurely.

With reference to Figure L,   point B is where a pilot would
experience an increase in airspeed; the plane may go above the
glideslope. Between points B and C, a pilot may reduce thrust in
order to reduce airspeed and return to the glideslope. Between
points C and D, the pilot discovers a sudden loss of airspeed and
the plane enters a rapid descent. It may be too late to increase
thrust and the airplane would contact the ground short of the
runway.

Figure K

Source: Federal Aviation Administration

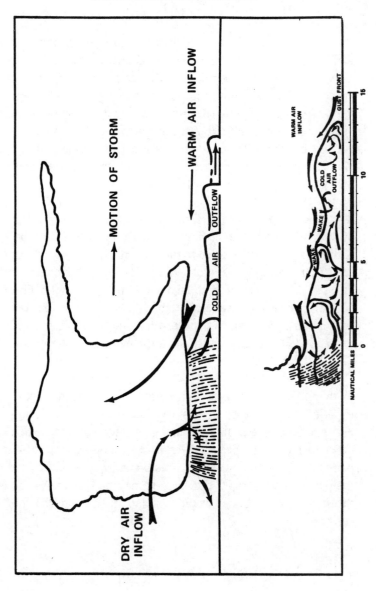

Figure L

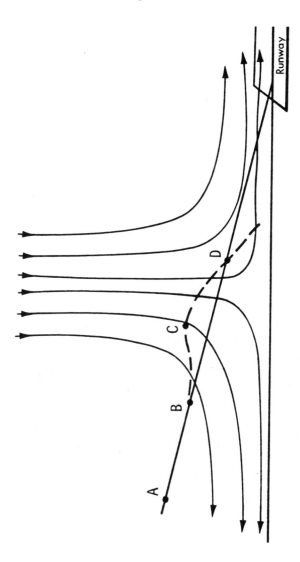

Source: Federal Aviation Administration

47

In the example I gave earlier, the airplane lost 20 MPH. It is possible for a plane to encounter several shears during the arrival or departure phase. Sometimes, the plane will suddenly lose airspeed, as I explained, or gain airspeed. The experienced pilot will accept a speed increase with the knowledge that it will be lost again shortly. It is common to suddenly gain airspeed and then lose it a few seconds later.

41)   Why do flights get cancelled?

A flight will be cancelled if the aircraft develops a mechanical problem that cannot be quickly repaired. Another reason is extremely bad weather. Air traffic control can stop everything for hours. A flight gets cancelled if the entire flight crew is not available to work. An example would be a pilot or flight attendant getting sick or injured. Crew scheduling will find a replacement (reserve crew member) and, depending on the circumstances, the flight might only be delayed.

The destination airport weather might be bad. We are not allowed to take-off unless the destination weather (visibility) is forecast to be at or above a certain value, typically one-half mile. Another possibility is that a runway is closed. There may be other runways available but unusable to your airplane due to the runway length, strong crosswind, or other operational restriction. The departure or destination airport may be closed due to an accident or special event.

Absolutely avoid the last flight of the day unless you're prepared to spend the night. Always try to have an alternate plan if your flight gets cancelled. You might be able to rent a car and go to another airport. Consider buses and trains. One time, we boarded a flight but air traffic control gave us a delay of one and a half hours. Then we boarded again only to have a cargo door break. It would be another two hours to fix it so the flight was cancelled. We had several passengers with international connections. They were now stuck because: 1) we were the last flight, 2) no other airline was flying to the destination, 3) it was too late to drive to another airport to try another flight, and 4) it was the end of the day so the airline had no flights it could divert to pick them up.

Had things gone smoothly, the international passengers would have arrived at the destination with three hours to spare before their connecting flight. Every once in a while, everything just goes down the tubes.

You also could have a problem in the morning. Don't think you can get the first flight and rush to a business meeting. If the flight is delayed or cancelled, you're stuck. It is also possible that your airplane didn't make it in the night before. You will get to the airport and not have an airplane. You could probably check that by calling the airline late the night before your flight. This is the one time when it's better for you to travel the night before.

42)   What causes delays?

The most common delay, for me, is caused by the volume of traffic. If several airlines schedule departures at the same time, then a traffic jam is inevitable. On more than one occasion I've been number 18 or greater for departure. One time, I was number 33.

Many airports use one runway for departures and another for arrivals. If a runway is closed, then the arrival aircraft have to be spaced apart more to allow room for departures. The departures will be spread out between arrivals. If the arrivals get backed up enough, the air traffic control system will not permit any more airplanes to depart for that airport. That is why your flight is sometimes held on the ground.

If the flight incurs a long delay, the airline may allow passengers to leave the airplane (I suggest you take your personal belongings with you). Do not leave the gate area. Air Traffic Control may suddenly release the flight and give the crew a small amount of time to get to the runway. The airline will round-up passengers but will not wait for everyone. The pilots must get to the runway by the time allotted by Air Traffic Control or risk a major delay. By the way, the pilots usually tell you everything they know, which is not much. The pilots can only repeat what is told by Air Traffic Control. Anything else is pure speculation.

Sometimes, a controller has to keep the aircraft on a particular airway (highway in the sky) spaced a certain number of miles apart. If there are aircraft on the airway when I'm ready to depart, the controller will hold me on the ground until there is room. The reason for the spacing is that many aircraft are arriving for the same airport during the same time period but from different directions. So, for example, an aircraft from the North gets in, then one from the South, then one from the West before the next aircraft from the North arrives. To put it another way, all the airplanes are spaced and staggered so as to arrive at the destination area in an orderly sequence.

Weather can cause massive delays. On nice days, pilots can indicate they have the airport or preceding aircraft in sight. The controller may clear the pilot for a visual approach and the pilot is then on his own. When the weather is bad (poor visibility), the controller has to guide the aircraft to the final approach course where the pilot then navigates to the runway. The controller gives the aircraft more space and that slows down the flow of traffic.

When thunderstorms are in the area, pilots have to deviate around them. This increases the controllers workload and flights can be slowed down. If there is a line of thunderstorms, it is like an impenetrable wall, and we will normally go to a holding pattern to wait for it to pass. Storms also play havoc with departures. Airplanes usually go to a *fix* (navigational location) after departure and then continue on their route. If a thunderstorm is at the fix, air traffic control may not permit departures to that area. If this happens to you, your aircraft will pull over or go to a holding area so other aircraft can get by and depart.

Snow also causes delays since runways and taxiways are occasionally closed to allow the pavement to be cleared. The de-icing procedure for aircraft is another source for delay.

A flight crew may have *timed out*. We are legally required to have a certain amount of rest before or after a work day. It is rather complicated but basically, if your morning flight is delayed for this reason, it means your crew got in late the previous evening. The Captain will refer to rest rules and determine they must have eight hours rest. The clock starts when the airplane parks. If the morning flight is less than eight hours away, it will be delayed until the crew has completed their rest period. By the way, the crew has eight hours to pack up, leave the aircraft, go to the front of the terminal, get a ride to the hotel, check-in, get ready for bed, sleep, get showered and dressed, get a ride to the airport, and reach the gate. Eight hours rest means six hours sleep or less. It's not much after a long day, but it's legal.

Maintenance also delays flights. It could be as simple as replacing a light bulb. If the aircraft was late arriving, it needs time to be fueled, cleaned, catered, and loaded with the out-bound baggage.

Generally speaking, flights are at the mercy of the air traffic control system and we are all at the mercy of weather. You should be prepared for disruptions to your schedule. A point to keep in mind is this: if your flight was delayed and arrives late due to air traffic control and/or weather, chances are your connecting flight also arrived late. Late arrivals mean late departures so you might still make your next flight.

If you arrive at the airport and learn your flight is delayed for a long time, do not go off to kill time in a store or restaurant. You should still go to the gate and try to learn what the situation is. You should check the monitors at least every 15 minutes. Here is a story to explain a typical problem.

You are going to Miami from gate 50. Your crew arrives on a Boeing 737 and parks at gate 10. They are now supposed to go to gate 50 and take that airplane to Miami. When they leave their airplane at gate 10, another crew takes it.

Your crew arrives to discover there is no airplane. It was delayed for weather in Chicago and will arrive 1 hour after you were supposed to leave for Miami. The airline will adjust the departure time on the monitor and will add about ½ hour for the airplane to be serviced.

At this point, everyone plans on being 1 ½ hours behind schedule. While some passengers disappear to eat, the airline discovers they have a spare plane at gate 25 that can be used. All of a sudden, your flight is scheduled to depart in ½ hour from gate 25. If you're off shopping or eating, you will not be aware of this and will return to the original gate to discover your flight has departed. If you must leave the boarding area, listen carefully to public address announcements and again, watch the television monitors frequently.

43)   How can I minimize the chances of my luggage being lost?

Check in at least an hour before flight time. This will give plenty of time for the luggage to be directed to the correct aircraft. Try to get a direct flight. Every time you make a connection, your luggage gets the chance to be misdirected. That's airline talk for *lost*.

If you do have a connection, your arrival time and next departure time should be at least an hour apart. That way, if your flight arrives a little late, your luggage should still have enough time to get to the next flight, and maybe you can walk instead of run to the gate.

Never pack items of high monetary or sentimental value in luggage that you plan to check-in. These items belong in your carry-on bag. Your carry-on bag should also contain one change of clothes and toiletry items. Spread your belongings among all the suitcases when you pack. That way, if a suitcase is lost, everyone loses a little instead of one person losing everything. Be sure to remove all tags and stickers from the luggage after you arrive at your final destination.

Buy good quality, hard shell luggage. It should have a strong handle and good locks. Luggage should always be locked, not only to prevent theft, but luggage will sometimes pop open from the shock of an impact. Never leave your bags unattended. Keep your leg against it so when you are looking around, you should be able to feel if the bag is moved. A confused visitor is an easy target. Always pack your own luggage.

I would not recommend putting your home address on the tag that goes on the handle. Anyone can read it and, knowing you are away, invite themselves over to steal your possessions. You might consider just a phone number of where you can be reached or the address of where you will be.

Finally, buy your luggage to do the job, not because it looks good. I've seen a white suitcase fall off a baggage cart into the snow and disappear -- far out on the ramp. Bags also fall out of carts at night. Buy bright colored luggage that stands out and put reflective tape around it.

Here's a special note if you fly on a small airplane or an *express* airline. There is a slight chance that your bag will not be loaded. Some airplanes, under certain conditions, will not be able to take all the luggage and all the passengers because of weight and balance limitations. Due to the high expense of losing luggage, an airline may elect to load all the bags and then remove some passengers. In reality, it's a lot easier and time efficient to leave bags behind. You can minimize your chances of this happening to you by checking your bag at the gate. This is not the same as checking your bag at the main airline ticket counter. When you check a bag at the gate, you are checking a bag that has been through security. Anyway, your bag should be waiting for you at the base of the stairs when you get off the plane. A gate check is like a carry-on you put in the baggage compartment. In most cases, this will work only with one or two bags that are the size of carry-on bags, in other words, small.

44)   How is my luggage processed?

Whether you check the bag at the curb or ticket counter, it will be tagged with the final destination ID and any applicable flight numbers. At a major airport, the bag arrives at a sorting area. All bags going to a particular destination (not necessarily the final destination) are placed together on a baggage cart. When departure time is near, the cart of bags is brought to the aircraft and loaded.   Depending on the aircraft, the bags may be individually loaded in the baggage compartment or placed in a bin which is then loaded in the aircraft.   On the Boeing 727, bag handlers usually stack the hard shell bags in one section and throw (literally) the soft luggage and garment bags into another.

At a small local airport, all the bags get on the same airplane. Upon arrival at the major airport, they are off-loaded and brought to the sorting area. They then go through the process explained earlier. If your connection is so close that you barely made it, there is a good chance your luggage didn't have enough time to be processed. If this happens, your bags will probably be put on the next flight.

Let's follow a bag which is being loaded at Elmira, New York for a trip to Lansing, Michigan.   At Elmira, it is tagged with the Lansing identification. It may also be given all the flight numbers for the route to Lansing (Elmira-New York, New York-Cleveland, Cleveland-Lansing).   At Elmira, all the bags will be going to different destinations, but going through New York. When the flight arrives at New York, all the bags will go to the sorting area. If New York is the final destination, the bag will be sent up to the appropriate carrousel for passenger pick up.   Our particular bag is going to Lansing by way of Cleveland, so it will be put on a baggage cart with bags going to Cleveland.   An airline may load all bags going through Cleveland together in one section of the plane and the bags that end in Cleveland in another.   This way, when the plane arrives, the baggage handlers take the batch of *through bags* to the sorting area and the other batch right to the terminal for passenger pick up.

Our bag has gone to the sorting area and is put on a baggage cart for the flight to Lansing. When it arrives at Lansing, all the bags will be off-loaded and brought to the terminal for passenger pick up.

Obviously, your bag is handled by many people. If one person misreads the destination tag, the bag can end up at a different destination than that intended. Another problem is that the baggage handler may read the tag correctly but puts it on the wrong baggage cart. It is important that you remove all tags and stickers from the previous time you traveled. If a ticket agent does it for you, he or she may miss one and your bag could end up at last year's vacation spot.

45)   Why do some airports seem to have a lot of airplanes from one airline?

Many airlines use the *hub and spoke* route system. That term is in reference to a bicycle wheel. The airline's center of operations, or *hub*, is where all the airplanes park to exchange passengers. Some hubs are: Atlanta (Delta), Dallas-Ft. Worth (American), Detroit (Northwest), Newark (Continental), Denver (United), and Philadelphia (USAir). If you're not at the hub, then you're at an *out-station*.

During the night, the airlines' aircraft are scattered among the outstations. In the morning, they will all fly into the hub. At this point, each inbound aircraft is carrying passengers who have different ultimate destinations. After the *arrival push*, the airplanes will all be serviced and the luggage sorted and re-loaded. At the same time, the passengers will get off their respective aircraft and board the flight going to their destination.

It's then time for the *departure push*. All the airplanes will head out to their destinations. The cycle begins again. They all fly back into the hub, exchange passengers and bags, and head out again for the out-stations. This *in and out* routine occurs several times a day and may lead to delays because of congestion.

Many airlines have at least three or four hubs in the United States. If you're at the Atlanta-Hartsfield airport, you're at a hub airport of Delta Airlines. You could go to just about any destination on them. If, however, you wanted to fly on another airline, you would likely have to travel to their hub first and then connect to another flight. Basically, you can go almost anywhere from the hub, but you have to get to the hub first.

46)   Sometimes, my ears bother me. How can I make them feel better?

The first step is prevention. You should not fly if you have a cold or congestion. The pain is caused by a difference in air pressure between the inside of your ear and the airplane cabin. As the airplane climbs, the cabin pressure may decrease to an atmosphere similar to 8,000 feet. The cabin pressure seldom remains at the pressure of the airport you departed.

If you have any congestion or blockage in the ear, you can end up with a bubble of trapped air in your ear. As the cabin pressure decreases, the pressure of the air in your ear appears to increase. This will cause you discomfort. Most people have no trouble with this since the air (and pressure) in your ear will eventually escape.

Getting the air back in your ear during descent is another story. If you had a tough time going up, you will probably experience an even tougher time going down. As the airplane descends, the cabin is pressurized to equal the atmosphere at the destination. As air pressure increases, you will feel discomfort because you have less air pressure in your ear. If it continues, the pain you feel can become great. Your inner ear will be like a vacuum and the surrounding membranes will be affected.

Normally, the following actions will minimize discomfort: swallowing, chewing, or yawning. For infants, crying is very good. If these don't work, your last hope is the Valsalva method. You must be very careful and gentle in its performance. Pinch your nose with your thumb and forefinger (like you're going under water). Take a breath (through your mouth) and then, very slowly and gently, build up pressure like blowing your nose. Don't be abrupt. This building of pressure will expand membranes in your ear and, hopefully, make an opening to allow air into your ear. Good luck!

47)   What is a missed approach?

The flying of the airplane is similar to a go-around (see question #20). The difference is a missed approach occurs, normally, during bad weather. It means the pilot flew a specific course to land at the airport and, at a designated point, did not see the runway or lost sight of it.

The most common approach is the Instrument Landing System. It guides the pilot up, down, left, and right, all the way to the landing portion of the runway. For many runways and airplanes, the pilot can descend to a point 200 feet above the ground. That's pretty low and is just a few seconds from landing.

If, at that point, nothing identifiable with the runway is in sight, the pilot must execute a missed approach. If the pilot sees something related to the runway, he can descend to 100 feet above the touchdown zone elevation. The Federal Aviation Regulations are very specific about the details.

Again, the airplane is flown as during a go-around but the pilot will comply with the missed approach procedure for that particular approach. It prescribes what altitude to climb to, the heading to fly, and where to navigate to. Many pilots might give the approach a second try before going elsewhere, but it depends on many factors.

48) How can a flight be cancelled due to poor visibility, and then the flight crew and plane take-off?

The Federal Aviation Regulations are very interested in protecting the traveling public. Airplanes carrying passengers for hire are operating under very strict rules, some of which dictate how much visibility is required for take-off. If the visibility is less than that prescribed, the flight will have to wait until conditions improve. An airline might decide to cancel the flight and send the plane and crew somewhere else.

If the flight is cancelled and the airplane carries no passengers, luggage or other revenue items, it can operate just like a private aircraft. Private planes operate under lenient rules (compared to airlines). They can take-off regardless of what the visibility is. At this point, it's up to the crew to decide if it's safe to attempt a take-off.

49) Why do planes get near the destination and then divert to another airport?

There are several possibilities. The airport may suddenly close due to an accident, evacuation of the control tower (happened to me once), arrival or departure of the President of the United States or other VIP, failure of a required navigational component during inclement weather, or some danger in the area. Perhaps the airport personnel need to plow snow from the runways.

Maybe, as happened to me once, the braking action was reported as nil. I can't land if the runway is an ice-skating rink.

A more common reason for diverting is when the weather suddenly and unexpectedly deteriorates to the point where the pilot cannot legally attempt an approach. Normally, a flight will not depart unless weather at the destination is forecast to be good enough to attempt an approach.

Last but not least, the airplane may develop a mechanical problem. There is a wide range of possibilities here. The airline may divert the flight to an airport with a maintenance facility. The pilots may need an airport with good weather and/or a long runway. The problem may be serious enough to require landing at the nearest suitable airport.

50)   How is my pet handled?

The handling of live animals probably varies from airline to airline. For starters, dogs for the visually impaired are normally allowed in the cabin provided they do not obstruct an isle or emergency exit. Small dogs and cats, in a travel cage, can usually be brought on board if they fit under the seat. You really need to check with the airline.

Other animals will have to be loaded with the luggage. Some airlines may supply a travel cage if you don't have one. Your pet will be handled like luggage but certainly should not get thrown around or have bags stacked on top.

The cage normally has a packet with it to identify the animal, owner, destination, and any special care instructions. The pet should be placed in a cargo bin which is pressurized and temperature controlled. The cage should also be secured with straps so it doesn't slide around.

The pilot receives a load manifest which will indicate the number of adults on board as well as children, infants, cargo or freight, baggage, and live animals. The Captain knows your pet is on board.

On some airplanes, the passengers and baggage are in the same overall compartment. That's to say the pressure and temperature is the same in both sections. On other airplanes, the baggage compartment may be completely separate and have its own pressurization and temperature control. One time, a Captain received an indication of a pressurization failure for a baggage compartment. He knew a dog was loaded there and would die before arrival at the destination. The Captain diverted the flight so the dog could be removed.

You should consult a veterinarian about air travel for your pet. Medication may be prescribed (for the pet) depending on the situation. Again, you should check with the airline to see what their requirements are.

WANT TO LEARN MORE?

There are many good books in the library. If you want to try flying an airplane, many airports offer an Introduction Flight. It's usually very inexpensive (maybe $30 or $40) and gives you a taste of what flight instruction would be like. Your local airport is a good place to start. If you want to take lessons, I would suggest you spend time just observing the instructors with students. You may select a particular instructor to give you lessons.

Flight instructors are normally young adults who are building flight time on their road to a flying career. You want to avoid an instructor that cares more about logging flight time than giving you quality instruction. If you have a personality conflict or trouble learning a particular maneuver, you might try a flight with someone else.

There are many older flight instructors who may have retired from airline flying and want to continue flying. The few that I knew often had interesting and amusing stories to tell about their airline and/or military days. They have a wealth of experience to share.

If you would like to write me, the address is: John Cronin, PO Box 1204, Edison, New Jersey 08818-1204.